Steve Bibisi

THE-IRS (THEIRS)

"You see, THE IRS thinks that your money is THEIRS, isn't it time we made it yours again"

This book is dedicated to Raymond Yakaitis,
who showed me that success is not just measured by the
bottom line, rather it is measured by the impact you
make and the lives you change.

10 Most Expensive Tax Mistakes That Cost Business Owners Thousands
(Updated for 2018)

Steve Bibisi

Kingdom Financial Solutions
1921 Boston Post Road
Westbrook, CT 06498
860.490.9741

The 10 Most Expensive Tax Mistakes That Cost Business Owners Thousands
Copyright © 2018 by Lucror, LLC

Contents

Kingdom Financial Solutions
1921 Boston Post Road
Westbrook, CT 06498
860.490.9741

Introduction

Are you satisfied with the taxes you pay?

Are you confident you're taking advantage of every available break?

Is your tax advisor giving you proactive advice to *save* on taxes?

If you're like most business owners, your answers are "no," "no," and "huh?"

And if that's the case, I've got bad news and I've got good news.

The bad news is, you're right. You *do* pay too much tax – maybe thousands more per year than the law requires.

You're almost certainly *not* taking advantage of every tax break you can. Our tax code is thousands of pages long, with tens of thousands of pages of regulations. There are thousands *more* pages of IRS guidance, along with volumes of court cases interpreting all those laws, regulations, and guidance. The sad reality is, there's probably no one alive taking advantage of *every* tax break they're entitled to, simply because there are so many of them out there.

And most tax advisors aren't very proactive when it comes to saving their clients' money. Sure, they get the "right" numbers in the "right" boxes on the "right forms," and getting them filed by the "right" deadlines. But then they call it a day. They do a fine job recording the history you give them. But wouldn't you prefer someone to help you *write* your own history?

The good news is, you don't have to feel that way. You just need a better plan. And you've already taken a giant step in that direction, whether you realize it or not. Owning your own business is the biggest tax shelter left in America. Now you just need to take advantage of what you already have!

In this book, we're going to talk about some of the biggest mistakes that business owners make when it comes to their taxes. Then we're going to talk about how you can *solve* those problems – legally and ethically.

I'm not here to make you an expert on taxes. Albert Einstein once said "the hardest thing in the world to understand is the income tax," and if taxes were hard for the guy who came up with the theory of relativity, it's OK if they're hard for the rest of us. You'll see the word "generally" a lot in this book, because the concepts are more important than the details or the exceptions.

My goal here is to ask some pointed questions and get *you* to look at your taxes with a new eye. You make choices about your tax bill every day. Are you making the *right* choices? Or are you like most business owners and professionals, leaving money on the table, wasting money on taxes you just don't have to pay?

Naturally, we'll talk about how the Tax Cuts and Jobs Act of 2017 affects these questions and strategies as well.

Supreme Court Justice Oliver Wendell Holmes once called taxes "the price we pay for civilization." But he never said we have to pay retail! This book will help you start finding discounts throughout your return.

1. Failing to Plan

#1 Mistake: Failing to Plan

> "There is nothing wrong with a
> strategy to avoid the payment of taxes.
> The Internal Revenue Code doesn't
> prevent that."
>
> ~William H. Rehnquist

The first mistake is the biggest mistake of all. It's failing to plan.

I don't care how good you and your tax preparer are with a stack of receipts on April 15. If you didn't know you could write off your kid's braces as a business expense, there's nothing we can do.

Remember the last time you drove a car? If you're like most people, you probably sat down in the driver's seat, strapped on your seat belt, turned the ignition, put the car in reverse, then backed your way to your destination, steering by what you could see out the rear view mirror.

Wait a minute… you mean that's not how you do it?

Why Tax Planning?

Well, that's how most tax preparers work. They spend lots of time looking back at what you did last year. But they don't spend much time looking forward. They can tell you all about what you did yesterday. But they don't tell you what you should do today, or when you should do it or how you should do it.

Tax *planning*, on the other hand, gives business owners like you two powerful benefits you can't get anywhere.

First, it's the key to your financial *defense*. As a business owner, you have two ways to put cash in your pocket. There's financial *offense*, which means making more. And there's financial *defense,* which means spending less. For most of you reading this book, spending less is easier than making more.

And for most of you reading this book, taxes are your biggest expense. So it makes sense to focus your financial defense where you spend the most. Sure, you can save 15% on car insurance by switching to GEICO. But how much will that really save in the long run?

Second, tax planning guarantees results. You can spend all sorts of time, effort, and money promoting your business – and that still won't guarantee results. Or you can set up a medical expense reimbursement plan, deduct the cost of your teenage daughter's braces, and guarantee savings.

But those guaranteed results start with *planning*. You can't ever deduct money you spend on a medical expense reimbursement plan if you don't set it up in the first place.

Now that we understand why planning is so important, let's take a quick look at how the tax system works. This will "lay a foundation" for understanding the specific strategies we'll be talking about soon.

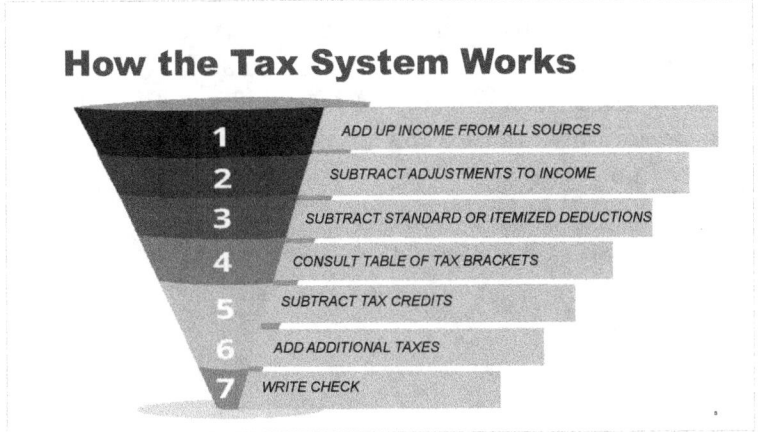

How the Tax System Works

1. ADD UP INCOME FROM ALL SOURCES
2. SUBTRACT ADJUSTMENTS TO INCOME
3. SUBTRACT STANDARD OR ITEMIZED DEDUCTIONS
4. CONSULT TABLE OF TAX BRACKETS
5. SUBTRACT TAX CREDITS
6. ADD ADDITIONAL TAXES
7. WRITE CHECK

- The process starts by adding up your income from all sources to calculate "total income."

- Next, you'll subtract a set of specific "adjustments to income" that are available to all taxpayers, whether you itemize or not.

- Next, you'll deduct your standard deduction or total itemized deductions, whichever amount is greater. Up through 2017, you also could deduct a personal exemption of $4,050 for yourself, your spouse, and any dependents.

- Next, you'll consult the table of tax brackets to determine your actual tax.

- Next, you'll subtract any available tax credits.

- Next, you'll add any extra taxes like self-employment tax or net investment income tax.

- Finally, you'll stroke a check to the IRS. If you've done a decent job with your withholding and quarterly estimates, you'll get a small refund. If you've done a *great* job, you won't owe anything *or* get anything back.

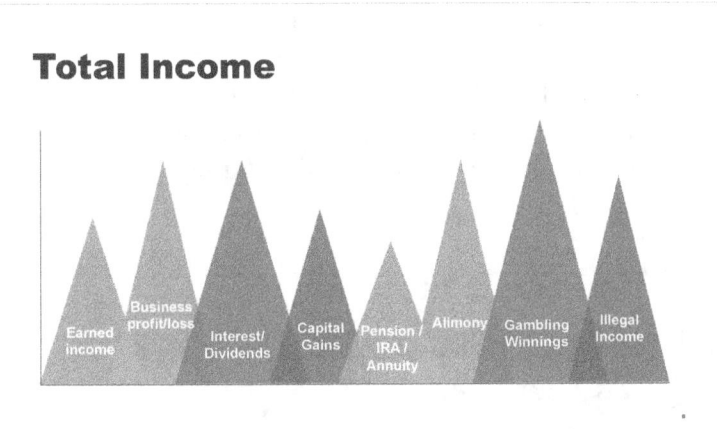

Total Income

The process starts with *income*. And this includes pretty much everything you'd think the IRS is interested in:

- Earned income from wages, salaries, bonuses, and commissions

- Profits and losses from your own business

- Interest and dividends from bank accounts, stocks, bonds, and mutual funds

- Capital gains from sales of property

- Income from pensions, IRAs, and annuities

- Alimony received

- Gambling winnings

Even illegal income is taxable. The IRS doesn't care how you make it; they just want their share! The good news, if you're operating most illegal businesses, is that you can deduct the same expenses as if you were running a legitimate business. For example, if you're a bookie, you can deduct the cost of a cell phone you use to take bets. The only exceptions include expenses "contrary to public policy" and most businesses involving illegal drugs.

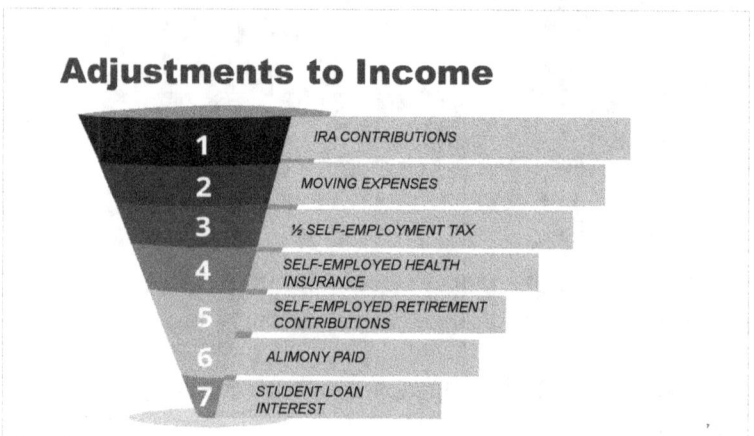

Adjustments to Income

1. IRA CONTRIBUTIONS
2. MOVING EXPENSES
3. ½ SELF-EMPLOYMENT TAX
4. SELF-EMPLOYED HEALTH INSURANCE
5. SELF-EMPLOYED RETIREMENT CONTRIBUTIONS
6. ALIMONY PAID
7. STUDENT LOAN INTEREST

Once you've added up total income, it's time to start subtracting "adjustments to income." These are a group of special deductions, listed on the first page of Form 1040, that you can take whether you itemize deductions or not:

- IRA contributions,

- Moving expenses (for active duty military personnel only starting in 2018),

- ½ of self-employment tax,

- Self-employed health insurance,

- IRA and self-employed retirement plan contributions,

- Alimony payments (for agreements entered into *before* January 1, 2019), and

- Student loan interest up to $2,500

Total income minus adjustments to income equals "adjusted gross income" or AGI. These are also called "above the line" deductions, because you take them "above" the line that separates total income from AGI.

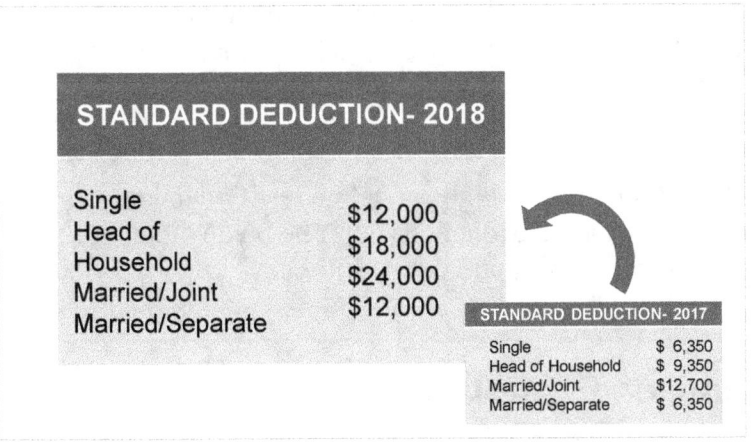

STANDARD DEDUCTION- 2018	
Single	$12,000
Head of Household	$18,000
	$24,000
Married/Joint	$12,000
Married/Separate	

STANDARD DEDUCTION- 2017	
Single	$ 6,350
Head of Household	$ 9,350
Married/Joint	$12,700
Married/Separate	$ 6,350

Once you've totaled your adjusted gross income, it's time to take your standard deduction or itemized deductions, whichever is more. And here's the first real change that most people will see after the Tax Cuts and Jobs Act of 2017. Standard deductions have essentially doubled. Those amounts were already high enough that about 2/3rds of taxpayers already take them. The new rules should drop that number to about 10%.

But there's a tradeoff that may cost you big-time. Remember those $4,050 personal exemptions? They're gone now. So, let's say you're a married couple, filing jointly, with no kids. For 2017, you received a $12,700 standard deduction and $8,100 in exemptions, for a total of $20,800. Suddenly that $24,000 standard deduction doesn't look *quite* so generous anymore.

If you're a married couple, filing jointly, with two kids, for 2017 you received a $12,700 standard deduction plus $16,200 in exemptions, for a total of $28,900 in tax-free income. Now that $24,000 standard deduction leaves you nearly $5,000 in the hole compared to where you were. The lower rates and expanded child tax credit may or may not make up that difference. But you should know that doubling the standard deduction may not be quite the gift it sounds like at first.

If your deductions are still high enough to justify itemizing, then the higher standard deductions don't help you – but losing your personal exemptions will still hurt.

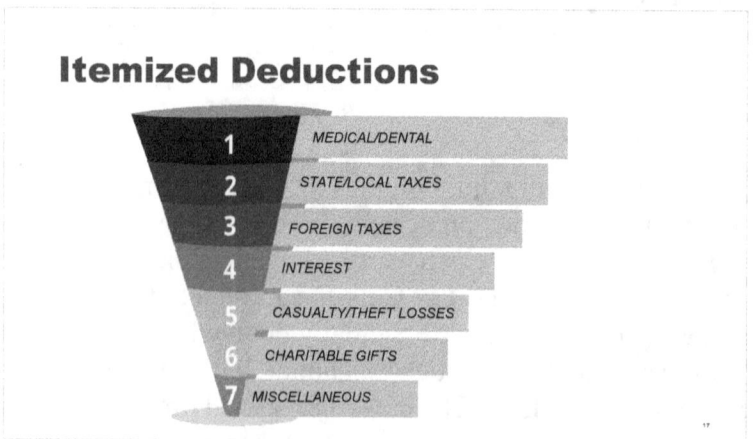

Itemized Deductions

1. MEDICAL/DENTAL
2. STATE/LOCAL TAXES
3. FOREIGN TAXES
4. INTEREST
5. CASUALTY/THEFT LOSSES
6. CHARITABLE GIFTS
7. MISCELLANEOUS

For those who benefit from itemizing, specific deductions include:

- Medical expenses, to the extent they top 7.5% of your AGI (this threshold goes up to 10% in 2019),

- State and local income, sales, and property taxes paid (up to a total of $10,000 per year, which is a new limit for 2018),

- Foreign taxes paid,

- Mortgage interest on up to $1 million for loans closed before December 15, 2017, or $750,000 for loans closed after that date,

- Casualty and theft losses incurred as a result of a federally-declared disaster, to the extent they exceed 10% of your AGI, and

- Charitable gifts.

Before the Tax Cuts and Jobs Act of 2017, you could write off a category of miscellaneous itemized deductions, to the extent they exceeded 2% of your adjusted gross income. These included employee business expenses, tax prep fees, and investment expenses. Those deductions are now eliminated. You also could write off interest on up to $100,000 of home equity interest you used for any purpose. That deduction is also now gone.

Tax deductions reduce your taxable income. If you're in the 15% bracket, an extra dollar of deductions cuts your tax by 15 cents. If you're in the 35% bracket, that same extra dollar of deductions cuts your tax by 35 cents.

Once you've subtracted deductions, you'll have your "taxable income." At that point, you'll consult the table of tax brackets to see how much to pay.

Tax Brackets: 2017

Rate	Single	Joint
10%	0	0
15%	9,326	18,651
25%	37,951	75,901
28%	91,901	153,101
33%	190,651	233,501
35%	416,701	416,701
39.6%	418,401	470,701

The chart above shows what tax brackets looked like in 2017. As you can see, there were seven brackets, starting at 10%, and rising to 39.6% on income over about a half a million dollars. Some people actually paid more than that 39.6% top rate if they owed self-employment tax or net investment income tax on top of their regular income tax.

Tax Rates Through History

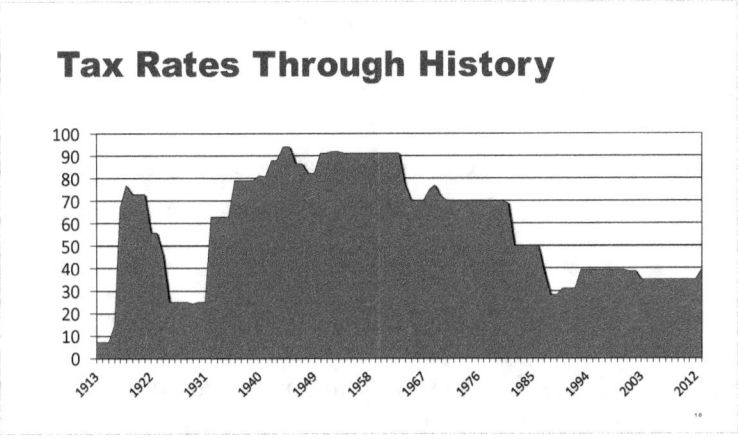

39.6% may sound like a pretty high top marginal rate, especially considering that it was just 35% until 2013. But today's rates are actually pretty low by historical standards. The very first income tax, in 1913, had a top rate of just 5% on income over $500,000 – that's about $12.6 million in today's dollars. But rates shot up quickly to pay for World War I, and went even higher to pay for World War II.

Tax Brackets: 2018

Rate	Single	Joint
10%	0	0
12%	9,526	19,051
22%	38,701	77,401
24%	82,501	165,001
33%	157,501	315,001
35%	200,001	400,001
37%	500,001	600,001

And here above is what the tax brackets look like for 2018. The Tax Cuts and Jobs Act keeps that same seven-bracket structure we had before, but cuts the rates.

Your bottom-line results here could be dramatic, or not, depending on how much you earn, how you earn it, where you spend it, and how many people you're supporting.

The changes in tax brackets are pretty obvious. But here's another important change that you won't see reflected on the chart. In 1985, Washington started indexing specific elements like standard deductions, personal exemptions, and tax brackets so that rising inflation wouldn't push taxpayers into higher brackets.

The IRS has traditionally used the Consumer Price Index, or CPI, to measure inflation. However, the new law specifies a different index, called the "chained" consumer price index. This index assumes that as prices go up, consumers react by choosing cheaper goods. For example, if the price of apples goes up, you probably won't stop eating them – but you might switch from Golden Delicious to Granny Smith. (If you're a millennial, substitute "avocado toast" for apples, and you'll get the point.)

The bottom-line result here is that that "chained" CPI rises more slowly compared to the regular CPI. The nonpartisan Tax Policy Center estimates that changing to chained CPI would increase taxes paid by 30% of the bottom quintile of the income distribution, 70% of the next quintile, and nearly all of the taxpayers in the top 60% of income. Bottom line, switching to chained CPI will function like a small but noticeable annual, across-the-board tax hike.

Tax Credits

1. FAMILY CREDITS
2. EDUCATION CREDITS
3. FOREIGN TAX CREDIT
4. GENERAL BUSINESS CREDITS
5. REAL ESTATE CREDITs

Finally, you'll subtract any available tax credits. These are dollar-for-dollar tax reductions, regardless of your tax bracket. So if you're in the 15% bracket, a dollar's worth of tax credit cuts your tax by a full dollar. If you're in the 35% bracket, an extra dollar's worth of tax credit cuts your tax by the same dollar.

There's no real secret to using tax credits, other than knowing what's out there. There are dozens available, but they fall into five main categories:

- Family credits, like the Child Tax Credit and Dependent Care Credit,

- Education credits, like the American Opportunity Credit and Lifetime Learning Credit,

- Foreign tax credits for taxes paid to foreign countries,

- General business credits for all sorts of business expenses, like research & development, hiring employees from disadvantaged groups, pension plan startup expenses, and the like, and

- Real estate credits, like the low-income housing credit and renovation credit.

The biggest changes in the tax credit category under the Tax Cuts and Jobs Act of 2017 involves the Child Tax Credit. Under the old rules, it was capped at $1,000 per child, up to age 16. The credit phased out by $50 for each $1,000 of "modified adjusted gross income" above $75,000 (single filers) or $110,000 (joint filers). (Modified adjusted gross income equals regular adjusted gross income, plus a seemingly random laundry list of items like nontaxable municipal bond interest, student loan interest, half of your self-employment tax, and any deductible college expenses.) If the credit was more than your actual tax bill, you might qualify for an "additional child tax credit" to the extent of any earned income above $3,000. (Sure makes you wish you could fill out your taxes on a postcard, right?)

The new law doubles the child tax credit to $2,000 per child. It raises the threshold for phasing it out to $200,000 for single filers and $400,000 for joint filers. It raises the age limit to 17. And it raises the refundable portion to $1,400, then indexes that amount for inflation.

Remember when we talked about those disappearing personal exemptions? The worst-hit taxpayers are the those with children. The new child tax credit rules should restore some of those lost benefits for those particular taxpayers.

The new law also provides a new $500 nonrefundable credit for dependents other than children. The rules here for claiming the credit are generally the same as they would be for claiming someone as a dependent.

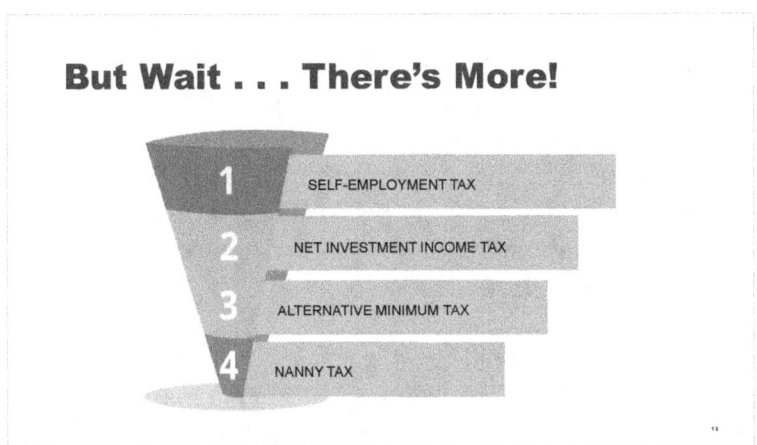

But Wait . . . There's More!

1 SELF-EMPLOYMENT TAX

2 NET INVESTMENT INCOME TAX

3 ALTERNATIVE MINIMUM TAX

4 NANNY TAX

We're not done yet! As the television infomercials say, "But wait . . . There's more!"

You may also owe self-employment tax, which replaces Social Security and Medicare taxes for sole proprietors, partnerships, and LLCs.

There's also a 3.8% net investment income tax on investment income, which "Obamacare" introduced in 2013. This tax hits single taxpayers earning more than $200,000 and joint filers earning more than $250,000. For purposes of this rule, "investment income" includes interest, dividends, capital gains, rental income, royalties, and annuity distributions.

Then there's "alternative minimum tax," or AMT, which requires you to throw out some of the most valuable deductions – like state and local income taxes – and recalculate your bill all over, using slightly lower rates but a bigger base. Which amount is higher, regular tax or AMT? Pay that one, thank you very much.

The new law raises the exemption amount (below which you're not subject to the tax) from $53,900 to $70,300 for single filers and from $83,800 to $109,400 for joint filers. It also increases the phaseout of those exemptions from $119,700 to $500,000 for single filers and from $159,700 to $1 million for joint filers. While this isn't nearly as good as *eliminating* the whole ridiculous travesty, it should protect millions of filers from its reach.

Finally, if you have household employees, you may have to pay a so-called "nanny tax" on their earnings. That may not sound like a big deal now. But it's definitely a big deal if you want to serve in the president's cabinet.

The bottom line here is that "tax brackets" aren't as simple as they might appear. Your *actual* tax rate can be quite a bit higher than your nominal "tax bracket."

So that's how the system works. (Easy peasy, right?)

Ultimately, there are two kinds of dollars in this world: pre-tax dollars, and after-tax dollars.

Pre-tax dollars are great, because you don't pay any tax on them. Earn a dollar, spend a whole dollar!

And after-tax dollars aren't *bad*. If you go to the grocery store to buy dinner for your family, the check-out clerk won't turn up her nose and say "sorry, we can't accept these *after-tax* dollars." But they're not nearly as good as pre-tax dollars, simply because you don't get to spend the tax you pay on them.

---

2. Audit Paranoia

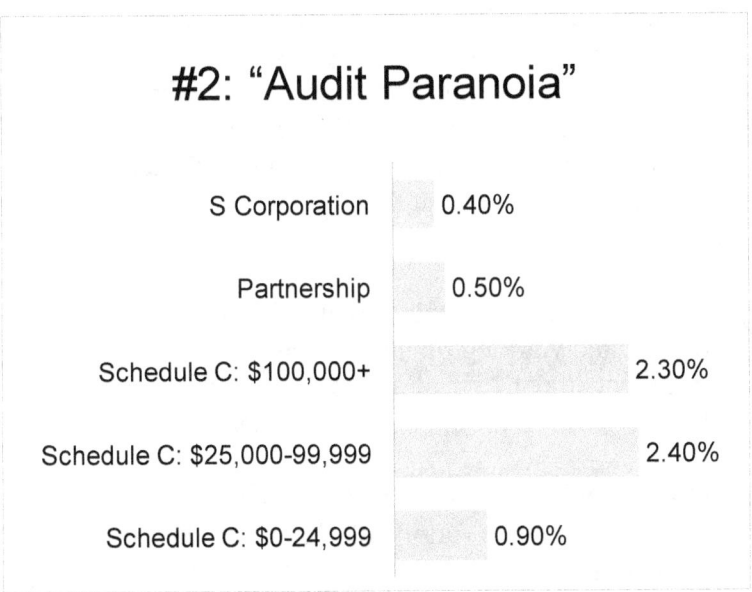

#2: "Audit Paranoia"

S Corporation	0.40%
Partnership	0.50%
Schedule C: $100,000+	2.30%
Schedule C: $25,000-99,999	2.40%
Schedule C: $0-24,999	0.90%

The second biggest mistake is nearly as important as the first, and that's *fearing*, rather than *respecting,* the IRS. Many business owners are simply afraid to take deductions they deserve, for fear of raising the proverbial "red flag."

But what does the kind of tax planning we're talking about really do to your odds of being audited? The truth is, most experts say it pays to be aggressive. That's because overall audit odds are so low, that most legitimate deductions simply aren't likely to wave "red flags."

Audit rates peaked in 1972 at one in every 44 returns. But lately they've dropped to historic lows. For 2016, the overall audit rate was just one in every 100 returns. Roughly half of those centered on a single issue, the Earned Income Tax Credit for low-income working families. The rest focused mainly on small businesses, especially sole proprietorships – and industries like pizza parlors and coin-op laundromats, where there are significant opportunities to hide income and skim profits. In fact, the IRS publishes a whole series of audit guides you can download from their web site that tell you exactly what they're looking for when they audit you!

So, if you *do* get audited, what then? Well, if you've properly documented your legitimate deductions, there's little to fear. In fact, about 15% of audits actually result in refunds. (Another 20% result in no change either way.)

And if you lose? You'll get what the IRS calls a "deficiency notice,' which is simply a bill for more tax. If you still think you're right, you can appeal it to the IRS. If you don't like the result you get there, you can appeal to the U.S. Tax Court. There's even a "small claims" division for disputes under $50,000.

Just how aggressive can you get before risking actual penalties (as opposed to merely paying more tax)? You can avoid accuracy-related penalties if you have a "reasonable" basis for taking a position on your return. Generally, this means your position has more than one chance in three of being accepted by the IRS. You can file Form 8275 or 8275-R to disclose positions you believe to be contrary to law or regulations. But some advisors recommend *not* filing them. Why volunteer information that can attract unwanted attention? (Think of this as the tax equivalent of calling in an airstrike on your own position.)

Are you worried about getting in *real* trouble, as in criminal prosecution? Don't. Seriously. For fiscal year 2016, the Service initiated just 3,395 criminal investigations. That's an almost unimaginably tiny fraction of the 240 million returns they collect in a year. Out of those investigations, they recommended 2,744 prosecutions (IRS investigators don't actually prosecute; they turn that job over to the Department of Justice.) There were 2,669 convictions leading to sentencing — the Feds don't take you to court if they're not already pretty sure they can win.

In the end, the average American really has nothing to fear from the IRS Criminal Investigations unit. As far as most of us are concerned, the IRS is just the government's collection agency, nothing scarier. You've got to do something pretty outrageous to draw one of those 3,395 investigations.

Sometimes, just changing how you report an item can dramatically change your odds of getting audited. Take a look at the chart at the beginning of this chapter. You'll see that for 2015, the IRS audited 2.3% of Schedule C businesses reporting gross income over $100,000. Yet for that same year, they audited just 0.5% of partnerships and 0.4% of S corporations, regardless of how much they made. That suggests you can cut your odds of being audited by over 80% just by reorganizing your business.

Here's the bottom line. You should never be afraid to take a legitimate deduction. And if your tax professional *does* recommend you shy away from taking advantage of a strategy you think you deserve, ask them to explain exactly *why* they say so. And don't be satisfied with a vague reply that it will "raise a red flag." Remember, it's *your* money on the table, not theirs.

3. Wrong Business Entity

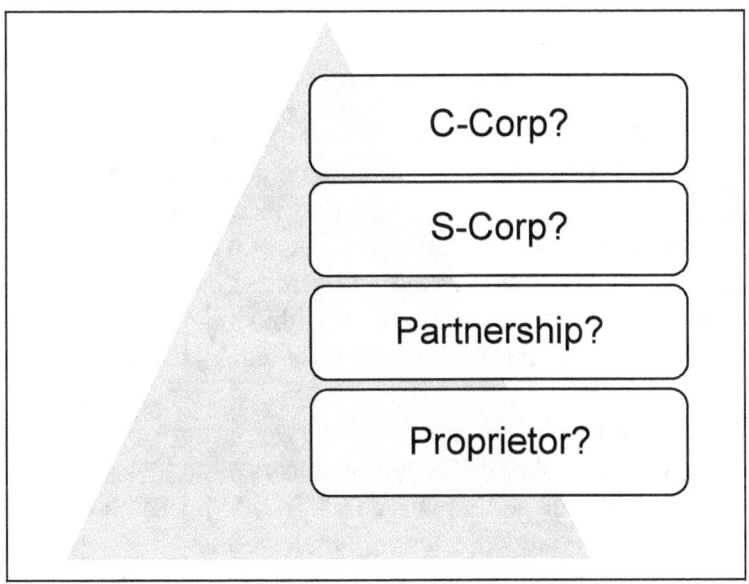

The next expensive mistake is choosing the wrong business entity.

Most business owners start as sole proprietors, then, as they grow, establish a limited liability company or corporation to help protect them from business liability. But picking the right entity involves all sorts of tax considerations as well. And many business owners are operating with entities that may have been appropriate when they were established – but just don't work as effectively now.

The Tax Cuts and Jobs Act makes this choice even more important by giving us a new deduction for "qualified business income." We'll talk about this more in the next chapter.

There are four ways you can organize your business:

- A **proprietorship** is a business you operate yourself, in your own name or a trade name, with no partners or formal entity. You report income and expenses on your personal return and pay income and self-employment tax on your profits. These are generally best for startups and small businesses with no employees in industries with little legal liability.

- A **partnership** is an association of two or more partners. General partners run the business and remain liable for partnership debts. Limited partners invest capital, but don't actively manage the business and aren't liable for debts. The partnership files an informational return and passes income and expenses through to partners. General partner distributions are taxed as ordinary income and subject to self-employment tax; limited partnership distributions are taxed as "passive" income.

- A **C corporation** is a separate legal "person" organized under state law. Your liability for business debts is generally limited to your investment in the corporation. The corporation files its own return, pays tax on profits, and chooses whether or not to pay dividends. Your salary is subject to income and employment tax; dividends are taxed at preferential rates. These are generally best for owners who need limited liability and want the broadest range of benefits. However, the administrative costs and complexities are also the highest.

- An **S corporation** is a corporation that elects not to pay tax itself. Instead, it files an informational return and passes income and losses through to shareholders according to their ownership. Your salary is subject to income tax and employment tax (Social Security and Medicare); pass-through profits are subject to ordinary income but not employment tax. These are generally best for businesses whose owners are active in the business and don't need to accumulate capital for day-to-day operations.

- Finally, a **limited liability company (LLC)** or **limited liability partnership (LLP)** is an association of one or more "members" organized under state law. Your liability for business debts is limited to your investment in the company, and LLCs may offer the strongest asset protection of any entity. However, a limited liability company is *not* a distinct entity for tax purposes. Single-member LLCs are taxed as proprietors, unless you elect to be taxed as a corporation. Multi-member LLCs choose to be taxed as partnerships or corporations. This flexibility makes LLCs the entity of choice for many startup businesses.

I can't make you an expert in business entities, not in a book like this. But I do want to walk through one popular choice to illustrate how important this question can be.

If you operate your business as a sole proprietorship, or a single-member LLC taxed as a sole proprietorship, you may pay as much in self-employment tax as you do in income tax. If that's the case, you might consider setting up an S corporation to reduce that tax.

If you're taxed as a sole proprietor, you'll report your net income on Schedule C. You'll pay tax at whatever your personal rate is. But (for 2018), you'll also pay self-employment tax, of 15.3% on your first $128,400 of "net self-employment income" and 2.9% of anything above that. You're also subject to a 0.9% Medicare surtax on anything above $200,000 if you're single, $250,000 if you're married filing jointly, or $125,000 if you're married filing separately.

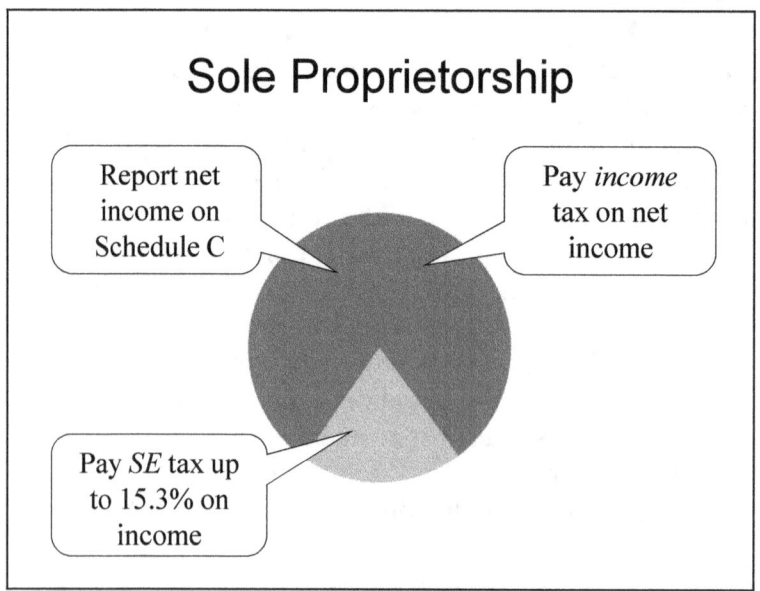

Let's say your profit at the end of the year is $80,000. You'll pay regular tax at your regular rate, whatever that is.

You'll also pay about $11,000 in self-employment tax.

That self-employment tax replaces the Social Security and Medicare tax that your employer would pay and withhold if you weren't self-employed. If you're like most readers, you're not planning to retire on that Social Security. You'll be delighted if it's all still there, but you're not actually counting on it in any meaningful way.

What if there was a way you could take part of that Social Security contribution and invest it yourself? Do you think you could earn more on your money yourself than you can with the Social Security Administration? Well, there is, and it's called an S corporation.

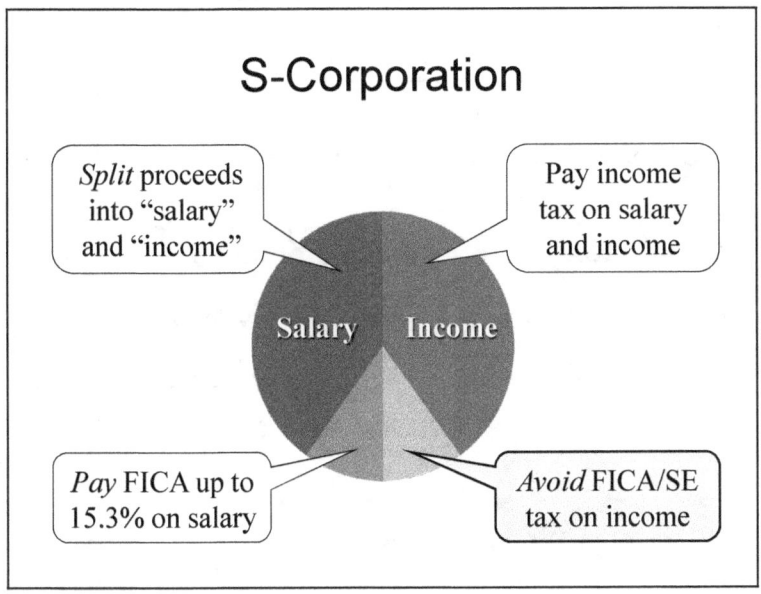

An S corporation is a special corporation that's taxed somewhat like a partnership. The corporation pays you a salary for the work you do. Then, if there's any profit left over, it passes the profit through to your personal return, and you pay the tax on that income on your own return. So the S corporation splits your income into two parts, wages and pass-through distributions.

Here's why the S corporation is so attractive.

You'll pay the same 15.3% employment tax on your wages as you would on your self-employment income. (You'll also pay the extra 0.9% Medicare tax on self-employment income exceeding $200,000 or $250,000, depending on whether you file alone or jointly.)

BUT – there's no Social Security or self-employment tax due on the dividend pass-through. And that makes a world of difference.

Employment Tax Comparison

S-Corp FICA		Proprietorship SE	
Salary	$40,000	Income	$80,000
FICA	$6,120	SE Tax	$11,304
Net	$73,880	Net	$68,696

**S-Corp *Saves*
*$5,184***

Let's say your S corporation earns the same $80,000 as your proprietorship. If you pay yourself $40,000 in wages, you'll pay about $6,120 in Social Security.

But you'll *avoid* employment tax on the income distribution.

And *that* saves you $5,184 in employment tax you would have paid without the S-corporation.

The best part here is that you just pay less tax. It's not like buying equipment at the end of the year to get big depreciation deductions. That may be a great strategy, but it also means spending something on the equipment to get that depreciation. It's not like locking money up into a retirement plan to get deductions. That may be another great strategy, but it also means you have to take money out of your budget to contribute to the plan.

Now, you still have to pay yourself a "reasonable compensation" for the service you provide as an employee – in other words, the salary you would have to pay to hire an employee to do the work for you. If you pay yourself nothing, or merely a token amount, the IRS can recharacterize up to *all* of your income as wage and hit you with some *very* hefty taxes, interest, and penalties. So don't get greedy! But according to IRS data, the average S corporation pays out about 40% of its income in the form of salary and 60% in the form of distributions. (And of course we can help you calculate that amount.) So you can see that there's at least a possibility for real savings.

4. Missing "Qualified Business Income"

Now let's talk about the biggest change the Tax Cuts and Jobs Act of 2017 makes for most business owners: a new kind of income from pass-through businesses.

Some background: the tax code has always recognized that there are different kinds of income – and treated those kinds of income differently.

Ordinary income is what you earn from your work or your business. If you earn a salary from a job, and your spouse loses money in a business, you can net those amounts against each other. If you draw pension or IRA income, that's ordinary income too. Ordinary income is taxed at ordinary rates.

Investment income is income you earn from your portfolio. And some of it, like taxable interest income, is taxed at ordinary income rates. But different kinds of investment income can be taxed at different rates. Qualified corporate dividends, for example, are taxed at special rates and capped at 20%. Long-term capital gains from property held for more than a year are also capped at 20%. And investment income is subject to a 3.8% "net investment income tax" if your AGI exceeds $200,000 for single filers or $250,000 for joint filers.

Now, if you have capital losses in a year, you can subtract them from your capital gains. And you can subtract up to $3,000 of net capital losses against your ordinary income. But if your net capital loss is more than $3,000, you have to carry the remainder forward to future years. So, to at least that extent, investment income is walled off into its own little silo.

By the mid-1980s, taxpayers had figured a way around that wall. They discovered they could use borrowed money to increase their basis in investments like real estate, oil & gas, and equipment leasing, and write off huge paper losses, well in excess of what they had actually invested. They used those losses to offset their ordinary income from salaries and businesses, as well as investment income from their investment portfolios. That was great for taxpayers, of course, especially with marginal rates hitting 70%. But it wasn't so good for the U.S. Treasury.

So, in 1986, Congress created a new category of income, called passive income, from activities where you don't "materially participate." The 1986 rules said that you can write off passive losses against passive income – but not generally against ordinary income or investment income. There's a rental real estate loss allowance for up to $25,000 of rental property losses, but *that* phases out starting at $100,000 of adjusted gross income. And so-called "real estate professionals" who qualify under special rules can deduct passive real estate losses against ordinary income. But for the most part, the 1986 rules walled off passive income and losses into a third silo.

Now Congress has created a fourth "silo," called qualified business income. Here's why they needed to do that. The Tax Cuts and Jobs Act lowered the top tax on C corporation income from 35% to 21%. That's a whole lot less than the maximum 37% tax on pass-through income from sole proprietorships, partnerships, and S corporations. To equalize the tax treatment between taxable and pass-through businesses, the Act defines the new qualified business income and lets you deduct 20% of that income, calculated on an activity-by-activity basis, from your taxable income for the year.

Qualified Business Income

QBI includes net business income from sole proprietorships, partnerships, and S corporations. It also includes pass-through income from real estate investment trusts, publicly-traded partnerships, and qualified agricultural coops. But it doesn't guaranteed payments or W2 wages you draw from your business. It also doesn't include investment income: most taxable dividends other than REITs, or coops, investment interest income, short-term or long-term capital gains, commodity or foreign currency gains, etc.

However, there are three important limits to this new deduction.

First, if your 2018 taxable income – *after* adjustments to income and itemized deductions – is over $157,500 ($315,000 for joint filers) your QBI deduction for each activity is limited to the greater of:

- 50% of the W2 wages timely paid on behalf of that activity, *or*

- 25% of the W2 wages plus 2.5% of the initial cost, immediately after acquisition, of all tangible property placed in service on behalf of that activity. (Tangible property includes real estate, equipment and machinery, vehicles, or robots that replace your employees.) You can count the initial cost of the property towards this amount for 10 years.

  Example: You own 20% of an S corporation that pays $500,000 in W2 wages and has $200,000 of property in service. Your QBI is the greater of $50,000 (50% of your 20% share of $500,000 in wages) *or* $26,000 (25% of your 20% share of $500,000 in wages plus 2.5% of your 20% share of the $200,000 in depreciable property).

This may mean that careful planning is required to maximize your deduction if your taxable income before subtracting QBI is enough to phase out the deduction.

Second, if your QBI comes from a "specified service business" (medicine, law, accounting, actuarial science, financial services, consulting, performing arts, athletics, or any business that relies on the "reputation or skill of one or more employees"), your deduction for that activity phases out as your taxable income rises from $157,500-207,500 (single filers) or $315,000-415,000 (joint filers).

This may mean that careful planning is required to define "specified service income" activities from non-service activities in order to make the most of the opportunity. (See below for more detail.)

Third, and finally, the overall QBI deduction is limited to 20% of your taxable income in any particular year.

(There's no provision for carrying over any unused deduction. However, if your QBI for the year is below zero, you can carry the loss forward to the next taxable year.)

The new rules suggest several ways to maximize the new benefit. And honestly, the more time tax lawyers and accountants spend looking over these rules, the more ideas they'll come up with. When critics of the tax bill say it will encourage "gaming the system," *this* is the provision they're talking about. *This* is ground zero for the games.

Create W2 Income

If you currently operate a non-service business as a sole proprietor or partner, you have few or no W2 employees, and your taxable income is above the $157,500/$315,000 threshold, consider establishing an S corporation and paying yourself a W2 wage to create a base for taking advantage of the deduction.

"Cracking and Packing"

Consider "cracking and packing" strategies to avoid the $157,500/$315,000 limits on specified service income.

If your primary activity is a specified personal service, consider "cracking" out ancillary activities, like marketing or management, into a separate activity. You'll still lose out on the deduction for that primary service activity. But you'll preserve the deduction for the ancillary activities that don't fall under the service business definition.

Alternatively, if part of your income comes from services, but a significant portion comes from elsewhere, you could "pack" non-service activities into a single entity so that it's *not* primarily providing services – and in that way, sidestep the service business limits.

Side Income

If you earn income from a side gig, on top of your primary business, consider segregating it into a separate activity. Let's say you throw passes for a pro football team. You probably also make income from endorsements. Your football salary won't qualify for the QBI deduction. But you can segregate your endorsement earnings into a separate entity to take advantage of the QBI deduction.

It's true that someday the IRS or Tax Court may rule that endorsements are a "specified service business" because they rely on "the reputation or skill of one or more employees." But why would you jump the gun and make that determination for them?

Segregate Real Estate

If you own real estate for your business to occupy, consider separating that real estate into a separate entity and paying it the highest reasonable rent to qualify for the deduction.

Ideally, you'll do this in the form of a real estate investment trust (REIT), because REIT pass-through dividends automatically qualify as QBI, no matter how much the REIT pays in W2 wages.

REITS have to have 100 shareholders. However, there are services available to help you find 100 preferred shareholders to invest $1,000 each in exchange for a $100 annual dividend. This gives them a sweet 10% return on their investment. And it lets you qualify for the attractive REIT tax treatment for a minimal $10,000 per year cost.

Contractors to Employees

If your business utilizes independent contractors, consider making them W2 employees to maximize the W2 base for calculating the QBI deduction. (Of course, if those contractors are *also* paying attention to the law, they may prefer to *keep* that status!)

Quit Your Job!

If you're working for the man, waking up to the noise of the alarm and trudging off to work every day to collect your pay, you're probably a little bit envious of your self-employed peers. They really could be doing the exact same work as you and paying tax on 20% less income, just because they run their own business.

So don't get mad, get even. "Quit" your job and join them!

Seriously . . . is there a way to renegotiate your relationship with your employer to become an independent contractor? If so, you'll immediately recharacterize your income in a way to take advantage of the new rules . . . as well as all the other planning opportunities available to business owners.

If you do find yourself able to renegotiate your relationship with your (soon-to-be-former) employer, be sure not to blow it when negotiating your pay. Don't just settle for your old salary – remember that your employer is also paying their half of your social security tax, and may be paying even more for healthcare coverage, retirement plan contributions, expense reimbursements, and other nontaxable benefits.

Final Notes on QBI

I realize this is going to sound self-serving. But this really isn't "do-it-yourself" planning. Just because you can buy a tool to do something yourself – instead of hiring a pro to use it – doesn't mean you should. If you go to Amazon and search for "orthopedic bone saw," you can find them for under twenty bucks. (Take a look. Seriously, it's terrifying!) But just because you can buy the tool, cheap, it doesn't mean you should be setting your kids' broken bones!

Want to hear something funny? Here's what the congressional conference committee responsible for final text of the Qualified Business Income provisions said in their report:

> *"It is not anticipated that individuals will need to keep additional records due to the provision. It should not result in an increase in disputes with the IRS, nor will regulatory guidance be necessary to implement this decision."*

Ha! Do you think they actually *believe* that? Or is it just something they told themselves to feel better about unleashing a hurricane of new uncertainty into the system?

5. Wrong Retirement Plan

Now let's talk about the fifth of our expensive mistakes: choosing the wrong retirement plan. As the chart below shows, the amount you can contribute at any income level varies widely according to which type of plan you have. If you make $90,000, for example, you can contribute $22,500 to a simplified employee pension (SEP), $14,700 to a SIMPLE IRA, and $41,000 to a 401(k). (And that's before any catch-up contributions you can start making at age 50.) But contribution limits aren't all you need to know. Which plan gives you the best combination of contribution, flexibility, and liquidity?

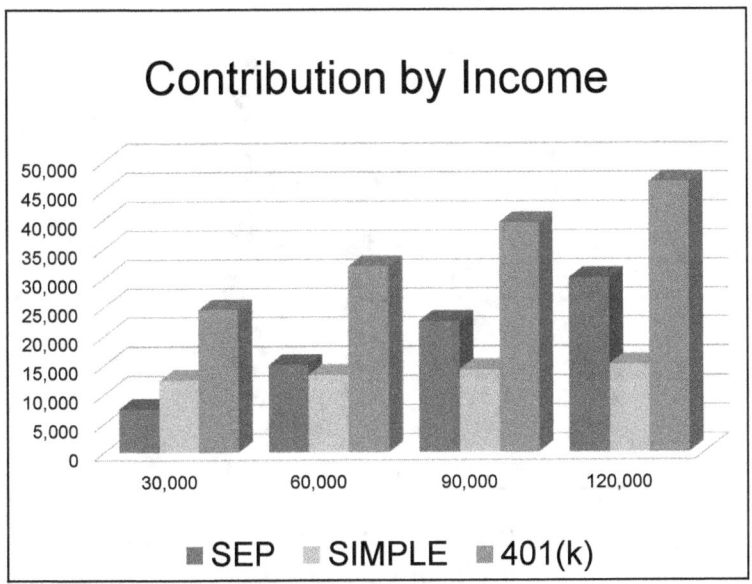

I'm not here to make you an expert on retirement plans. But I *can* help you decide pretty quickly if the plan you have is right for you – or if you should be looking for something more suited for your specific needs. So bear with me, even if the next few pages look intimidating. These are some very powerful strategies.

We'll assume for the purposes of this discussion that you've already decided you want to save more than the $5,500 you can save in an IRA. We'll also assume, at least for the next few pages, that you want a "traditional" arrangement, where you deduct the contributions you make now and pay tax on withdrawals. (We'll address alternatives, including Roth arrangements and life insurance, towards the end of the chapter.)

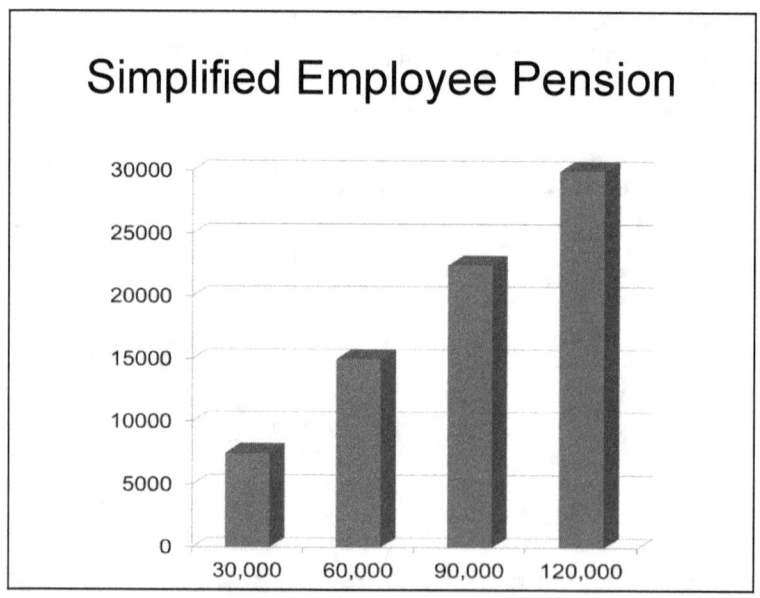

Simplified Employee Pension

The Simplified Employee Pension, or "SEP," is the easiest plan to set up because it's just a turbocharged IRA:

- If you're self-employed, you can contribute up to 25% of your "net self-employment income."

- If your business is incorporated and you're salaried, you can contribute 25% of your "covered compensation," which essentially means your salary.

- The maximum contribution for any single employee in 2018 is $55,000.

- If you've got employees, you'll have to contribute for them, too. You generally have to contribute the same percentage for your employees as you do for yourself. However, if your income is significantly higher than that of your employees, you can use what's called an "integrated" formula to make extra contributions for higher income earners.

- The money goes straight into regular IRA accounts you set up for yourself and your employees. There's no annual administration or paperwork required.

- SEP assets accumulate tax-deferred over time. You'll pay tax on them at ordinary income rates when you withdraw them in retirement. There are penalties for early withdrawals before age 59½, and for failing to take required minimum distributions beginning at age 70½.

The SEP is easy to adopt, easy to maintain, and flexible. If there's no money to contribute, you just don't contribute. But remember, the contribution is limited to a percentage of your covered compensation. So, for example, if you set up an S corporation to limit your self-employment tax, you'll also limit your SEP contribution because it's based on that lower salary amount.

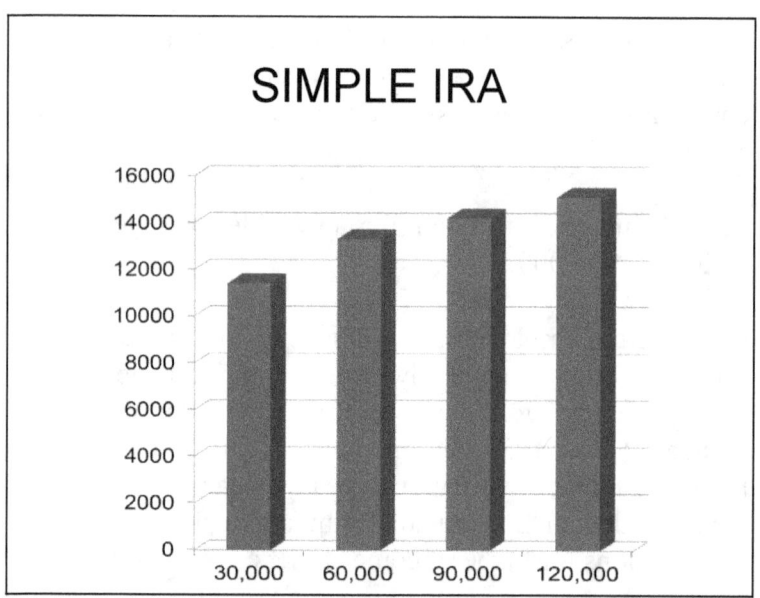

SIMPLE IRA

The next step up the retirement plan ladder is the SIMPLE IRA. This is another "turbocharged" IRA that lets you contribute more than the usual $5,500 limit:

- You and your employees can "defer" and deduct 100% of your income up to $12,500.

- If you're 50 or older you can make an extra $3,000 "catch up" contribution.

- But – you have to match everyone's deferral or make profit-sharing contributions. You can match employee contributions dollar-for-dollar up to 3% of their pay, or contribute 2% of everyone's pay whether they choose to defer or not. If you choose the match, you can reduce it as low as 1% for two years out of five.

- The money goes straight into employee IRAs. You can designate a single financial institution to hold the money, or let your employees choose where to hold their accounts.

- There's no set-up charge or annual administration fee for the plan. You're simply establishing special IRAs for your employees. You're not establishing a qualified plan trust to hold the assets like you would with a 401(k) or defined benefit plan.

- SIMPLE assets accumulate tax-deferred over time. You'll pay tax at ordinary income rates when you withdraw them in retirement. There are penalties for early withdrawals before age 59½, and failing to take required minimum distributions beginning at age 70½.

The SIMPLE IRA may be best for part-time or sideline businesses earning less than $50,000, because the flat $12,500 contribution is higher than the 25% SEP contribution for incomes up to $50,000. And it may be best for lower-paid employees. The maximum contribution is below the $18,500 limit for a 401(k). But how many of your employees will actually contribute that maximum amount anyway?

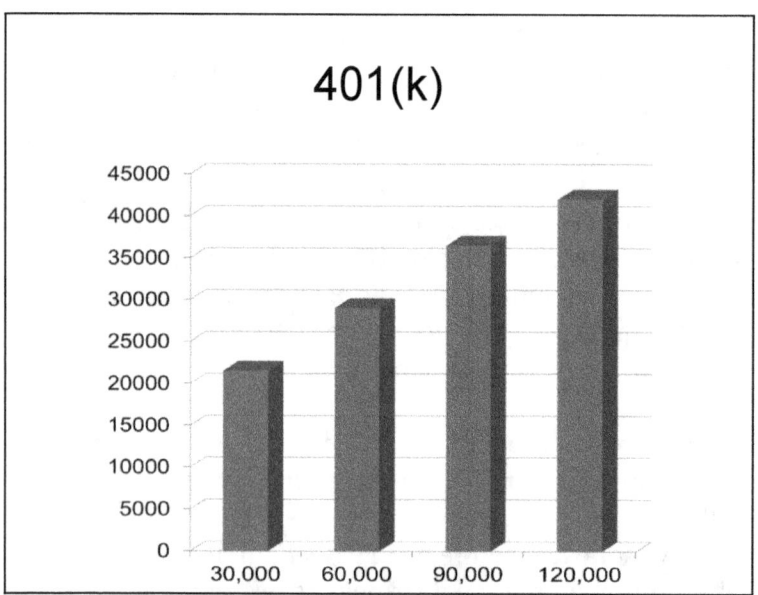

401(k)

The next step up the retirement plan ladder is the 401(k).

Most people think of 401(k)s as retirement plans for bigger businesses. But you can set up a 401(k) for any size business. In fact, you can even set up what's called a "solo" or "individual" 401(k) just for yourself.

The 401(k) is a true "qualified" plan. This means you'll set up a trust, adopt a written plan agreement, and choose a trustee. But the 401(k) lets you contribute far more money, far more flexibly, than either the SEP or the SIMPLE.

- You and your employees can "defer" and deduct 100% of your income up to $18,500 for 2018. If you're 50 or older, you can make an extra $6,000 "catch up" contribution.

- You can choose to match contributions, or make "profit-sharing" contributions up to 25% of everyone's pay. (If you operate as an S corporation, you can contribute up to 25% of your salary, but not any pass-through distributions.) That's the same percentage you can save in your SEP – *on top of* the $18,500 deferral.

- The maximum contribution for 2018 is $55,000 per person, plus any "catch up" contributions.

- You can offer yourself and your employees loans, hardship withdrawals, and all the bells and whistles "the big boys" offer their employees.

- You can use "cross-testing" to skew profit-sharing contributions to favored employees. "Age-weighted" plans allocate more to older employees (on the theory that they have less time to save for retirement); "integrated" and "super-integrated" plans allocate more to higher-paid employees (on the theory that they get no benefit from Social Security for their income above the Social Security wage base); and "rate group" plans divide employees into groups (such as managers, administrators, and salespeople) and make different contributions for each group.

- 401(k) assets accumulate tax-deferred over time. You'll pay tax at ordinary income rates when you withdraw them in retirement. There are penalties for early withdrawals before age 59½, and failing to take required minimum distributions beginning at age 70½.

The downside? 401(k)s are true "qualified" plans, which means more administration than SEPs or SIMPLEs. You'll have to file Form 5500 reporting contributions and assets, every year. And there are complicated anti-discrimination and "top-heavy" rules to keep you from stiffing your employees while you stuff your own account.

However, if the 401(k) really *does* make sense, there are three alternatives that might make administration easier:

- A "SIMPLE" 401(k) avoids nondiscrimination and top-heavy rules in exchange for guaranteed employer contributions. You and your employees can defer 25% of covered compensation up to the SIMPLE plan contribution limits. Your business has to contribute 2% of covered comp or match contributions up to 3% of covered comp. This works if you want a true 401(k), but you're afraid your employees won't contribute enough to let *you* make meaningful deferrals. You can also convert an existing 401(k) to a SIMPLE 401(k).

- A "Safe Harbor" 401(k) avoids nondiscrimination (but not top-heavy) rules in exchange for bigger employee contributions. You and your employees can defer up to the regular 401(k) limit. You can either: 1) contribute 3% of covered comp; or 2) match contributions dollar-for-dollar up to 3% of covered comp and fifty-cents-on-the-dollar for contributions between 3% and 5% of covered comp. You can even make extra profit sharing contributions on top of the required contributions.

- If you operate your business all by yourself, with no employees other than your spouse, you can establish an "individual" 401(k) with less red tape.

Finally, if you want to contribute more than the $55,000 limit for SEPs or 401(k)s, you might consider a defined benefit plan. This is your father's retirement plan – the traditional "pension plan" that so many employers have stopped offering because they can't afford it anymore. However, it can still be a great choice for older, highly compensated business owners with few employees.

Defined Benefit Contributions		
Age	Regular DB	412(i)
45	$80,278	$164,970
50	$133,131	$258,019
55	$211,448	$395,634
60	$236,910	$450,112

Projections based on retirement at age 62 with $165,000 annual pretax income.

- Defined benefit plans let you guarantee up to $220,000 in annual income (2018 limit).

- You can contribute – and deduct – as much as you need to finance that benefit. You'll calculate those contributions according to your age, your desired retirement age, your current income, and various actuarial factors.

- A 412(e) plan (previously called a 412(i) plan), which is funded entirely with life insurance or annuities, lets you contribute even more.

The biggest problem with the defined benefit plan is the required annual contributions. If your business doesn't have the money, you still have to pay. However, you can combine a defined benefit plan with a 401(k) or SEP to give yourself a little more flexibility. Let's say you could contribute up to $100,000 to a defined benefit plan, but you're not confident you can commit to that much every year. You might set up a defined benefit plan with a $50,000 contribution, then pair it with 401(k) for another $50,000. If business is poor in a particular year, you can choose to skip the 401(k) that year.

So, now that we've covered the menu of traditional employer-sponsored retirement plans, let's throw another wrench into the mix. Do you even want or need a traditional plan? Or would you be better off with an alternative? Perhaps even giving up the current tax break?

All of the plans we've discussed so far assume that you're better off taking a tax deduction for plan contributions now, as they go in the plan, then letting plan assets accumulate tax-free over time, and then paying tax on withdrawals, at ordinary income rates, when you need them for retirement.

That's a great strategy if your tax rate is higher now than it will be in retirement. You benefit now by avoiding tax on contributions, which puts more to work for you today. And you benefit later by paying less tax on withdrawals.

But that traditional pattern doesn't always hold true. (Remember the graphic charting marginal tax rates we saw back in Chapter One?) Maybe you're young, just starting your career, and your income is low. Maybe you're transitioning from one career or business to another, and your income is temporarily low. Maybe you think that tax rates in general will rise. (Today's top marginal rate may seem high at 37%, but that's actually quite low by historical standards.) Sometimes, contributing to a traditional retirement plan creates a ticking tax time bomb and actually *costs* you money over the long run.

Here are two alternatives you might consider if standard qualified plans don't fit the bill:

- "Roth" accounts take the traditional defer-now, pay-later arrangement and turn it on its head. The basic Roth IRA doesn't give you any deduction for contributions you make today. But your withdrawals are generally tax-free so long as they've "aged" at least five years. Tax-free income sounds great, right? However, contributions are limited to $5,500 per year ($6,500 if you're 50 or older), and you can't contribute at all if your income is over $135,000 (single filers) or $199,000 (joint filers). (If your income is above those limits, you can still fund a Roth by contributing the maximum to a nondeductible traditional IRA, then immediately convert it to a Roth.)

  If you sponsor a 401(k), you can choose to designate your salary deferrals up to $18,500 as

"Roth" deferrals. You won't get any deduction today, but your withdrawals down the road will be tax-free. (Any employer contributions will continue to be treated as deductible now and taxable later.)

If you have a SEP, you can create a backdoor "Roth SEP" by making a deductible SEP contribution, then immediately converting it to a Roth. Roth conversions in general are a subject for another book – I just want you to be aware that the possibility exists. (You can do the same thing with a SIMPLE, but you have to wait at least two years from the time you contribute the money until the time you convert it to a Roth.)

- Permanent life insurance policies that include a cash value can offer several significant tax breaks for supplemental retirement savings. There's no deduction for premiums you pay into the contract. But policy cash values grow tax-deferred. And you can take cash from your policy, tax-free, by withdrawing your original premiums and then borrowing against remaining cash values. You'll pay (nondeductible) interest on your loan, but earn it back on your cash value. Many insurers offer "wash loan" provisions that let you borrow against your policy with little or no out-of-pocket costs.

These advantages aren't completely unlimited. If you stuff too much cash into the policy in the first seven years, it's considered a "modified endowment contract" and all withdrawals are taxed as ordinary income until you exhaust your inside buildup.

Insurers offer three main types of cash-value policies with three different investment profiles to suit different investors. The key is finding a policy that matches your investment temperament:

> "Whole life" resembles a bank CD in a tax-advantaged wrapper, with required annual premiums and strong guarantees. Remember when we said the defined benefit pension was your father's pension plan? Well, this is your father's life insurance.

> "Universal life" generally resembles a bond fund in a tax-advantaged wrapper, with flexible premiums but less strong guarantees. Some insurers also offer "indexed universal life," which lets you profit from equity markets but give you a guaranteed return even when those markets are down.

> "Variable life" lets you invest cash values in a series of "subaccounts" resembling mutual funds in a tax-deferred wrapper. You can choose "variable whole life" with required premiums and stronger guarantees, or "variable universal life" contracts with flexible premiums and less strong guarantees.

Once again, I'm not here to make you an expert in retirement plans or alternatives. My goal is simply to open your eyes to the wide variety of plans and options so that you can evaluate if the plan you have now is really the right plan for you. I also want to keep you from falling into the common trap of assuming that deferring today's income is always the right retirement planning strategy.

6. Missing Family Employment

Now let's talk about the sixth mistake: missing family employment. Hiring your children and grandchildren can be a great way to cut taxes on your income by shifting it to someone who pays less.

- Yes, there's a minimum age. They have to be at least seven years old.

- Their first $12,000 of earned income is taxed at zero. That's because $12,000 is the standard deduction for a single taxpayer – even if you claim them as your dependent. Their next $9,525 of taxable income is taxed at just 10%. That may be more income than you would have expected you would be able to shift downstream.

- You have to pay a "reasonable" wage for the service they perform. The Tax Court says this is what you'd pay a commercial vendor for the same service, with an adjustment made for the child's age and experience. So, if your 12-year-old cuts grass for your rental properties, pay him what a landscaper might charge. If your 15-year-old helps keep your books, pay him a bit less than a bookkeeping service might charge. Does anyone have a teenager who helps with your web site? What would you pay a commercial designer for that service?

- To audit-proof your return, write out a job description and keep a timesheet.

- Pay by check, so you can document the payment.

- You have to deposit the check into an account in the child's name. But it doesn't have to be his pizza-and-Nintendo fund. It can be a Roth IRA for decades of tax-free growth. It can be a Section 529 college savings plan. Or it can be a custodial account that you control until they turn 21. Now, you can't use money in a custodial account for your obligations of parental support. But private and parochial school aren't obligations of parental support. Sleepaway summer camp isn't an obligation of parental support.

Let's say your teenage daughter wants to spend two weeks at horse camp. You can earn the fee yourself, pay tax on it, and pay for camp with after-tax dollars. Or you can pay her to work in your business, deposit the check in her custodial account, and then, as custodian, stroke the check to the camp. Hiring your daughter effectively lets you deduct her camp as a business expense.

Here's another little bonus you'll like. If you hire your child to work in an unincorporated business, you don't have to withhold for Social Security until they turn 18. So this really is tax-free money. You'll still have to jump through some paperwork hoops, like issuing a W-2 at the end of the year and reporting their income on their own return if the income is enough to require them to file themselves. But this is painless compared to the tax you'll waste if you don't take advantage of this strategy.

Finally . . . just *maybe* . . . hiring your kids to actually work for you might teach them a thing or two about the value of a dollar.

7. Missing Medical Benefits

Now let's talk about health-care costs. Surveys used to show that taxes *used to be* small business owners' biggest concern. Now it's rising health care costs.

If you pay for your own health insurance, you can deduct it as an adjustment to income on Page 1 of Form 1040. If you itemize deductions, you can deduct unreimbursed medical and dental expenses on Schedule A, *if* they total more than 7.5% of your adjusted gross income. But most of us just don't spend that much on our healthcare. So we wind up losing thousands in otherwise legitimate deductions.

What if there was a way to write off medical bills as business expenses? There is, and it's called a Medical Expense Reimbursement Plan, or Section 105 Plan.

"Employee" Benefit Plan

Sole Proprietorship	Hire Spouse
Partnership	Hire Spouse (if <5% owner)
C-Corporation	Hire Self
S-Corporation	>2% Shareholders/ Spouses Ineligible

The first thing you need to know about a MERP is that it's an *employee* benefit plan. That means (spoiler alert) it requires an employee:

- If your business is taxed as a sole proprietorship, you're considered self-employed. You can't establish the plan for yourself. However, if you're married, you can hire your spouse.

- If your business is taxed as a partnership, you're also considered self-employed. Again, you can't establish the plan for yourself. However, you can still hire your spouse so long as he or she owns less than 5% of the business.

- If your business is taxed as an S corporation, both you and your spouse are considered self-employed. This means you'll need another source of income, not taxed as an S corporation, to establish the plan. (Alternatively, you can establish a health savings account, which we'll discuss in a few pages, to give yourself most of the same benefit as the 105 plan.)

- If your business is taxed as a "C" corporation, you qualify as your own employee, so you can simply hire yourself.

If you're married, and you choose to hire your spouse, you don't even have to pay him or her a salary. You can compensate them in the form of benefits only, which avoids the hassle of filing payroll returns. The main requirement here is that the benefits you pay have to be "reasonable compensation" for the service they perform. If your spouse works an hour a month filing invoices for you, you'll probably have a hard time convincing an auditor that that's "reasonable" for $4,000 worth of LASIK surgery!

Eligible Expenses

- Major medical, LTC, Medicare, "Medigap"
- Co-pays, deductibles, prescriptions
- Dental, vision, and chiropractic
- Braces, fertility treatments, special schools
- Nonprescription medications and supplies

Once the plan is in place, you can reimburse your employee for any medical expense they incur for themselves, their spouse, and their dependents.

- This includes any kind of health insurance, including major medical, long-term care (up to specific IRS limits), Medicare premiums, and even Medigap coverage.

- It includes all your copays, deductibles, "co-insurance,' and other amounts insurance doesn't pay.

- It includes all your prescription drugs.

- It includes expenses for things like dental care, vision care, and chiropractic care that traditional insurance might not cover.

- It includes some really "big-ticket" items like braces for your kids' teeth, fertility treatments, and special schools for learning-disabled children. Let's say your physician diagnoses your 8-year-old son with ADHD, and prescribes *tai kwon do* lessons. Guess what – those lessons are now tax-deductible!

- It even includes over-the-counter medications and supplies, so long as they're actually prescribed by a physician.

One big advantage of the MERP is that it works with any insurance policy. You don't have to buy special coverage. You can use a MERP with insurance you buy on your own or insurance you buy through an exchange. If your spouse gets coverage from their employer, you can even set up a MERP in your business to cover whatever out-of-pocket expenses your spouse's insurance doesn't cover.

Let's assume you're a sole proprietor with two kids and you've hired your husband to work for your business. The plan lets you reimburse your husband/employee for all medical and dental expenses he incurs for himself – his spouse (which brings you into the plan) – and *his* dependents, your kids.

This includes all the expenses listed above.

The best part is, this is money you'd spend anyway, whether you got a deduction or not. You'll spend your money on glasses or your kids' braces whether it's deductible or not. The MERP just lets you move it from someplace on your return where you certainly can't deduct all of it (and probably can't deduct *any* of it), to a place where you can.

The "Paperwork"

- Written plan document
- Verify bona fide employment
- Benefits = "reasonable compensation"
- Document payments
- Third-party administrator?

Okay, how do you make it work? Well, for starters, you'll need a written plan document. (We can help with that.)

If you've hired your spouse, you'll need to be able to verify that they qualify as a bona fide "employee." That means you need to direct the work they perform for the business, the same as you would direct the work that any other employee performs.

Here's one important requirement that the IRS *will* pay attention to in the unlikely event you get audited. You *do* have to run the payments through the actual business. You can't just pay medical bills out of the family personal account, total them up at the end of the year, and throw them on the business return.

This means you have two choices. You can pay health-care providers directly out of the business account. Or you can reimburse your employees for expenses they pay out of

their personal funds. Let's say your husband needs to pick up a prescription. He can use his own money, and you can reimburse him. Or he can use a business credit card and charge it to the business directly.

There's generally no need for an outside third-party administrator, or "TPA," if you've simply hired your spouse to write off your own family's medical expenses. However, you will need a TPA if you're reimbursing nonfamily employees in order to avoid violating medical privacy rules.

There's no pre-funding required. You don't have to open a special bank or investment account, like with Health Savings Accounts or flex-spending plans. You don't have to decide up front how much you want to contribute to the plan, like you do with flexible spending accounts, and there's no "use it or lose it" rule. The MERP is really just an accounting device that lets you recharacterize your family medical bills as a business expense.

The MERP doesn't just help you save *income* tax. It also helps you save *self-employment* tax. Remember, when you work for yourself, you pay a special self-employment tax, which replaces the Social Security and Medicare taxes that you and your employer would share on your salary. That self-employment tax is based on your "net self-employment earnings" – but when you set up a MERP, the deduction reduces that self-employment income.

MERP Requirements

- Must cover "eligible employees"
- Exclusions
  - Under age 25
  - Under 35 hours/week
  - Under 9 months/year
  - Under 3 years service
  - Collective bargaining agreement
- Excise tax on Form 720

Now, here's the bad news. If you have non-family employees, you have to include them too. Now, you can exclude employees under age 25, who work less than 35 hours per week, less than nine months per year, or who have worked for you less than three years. You can also exclude employees covered by a collective bargaining agreement that includes health benefits. But still, having non-family employees may make it too expensive to reimburse everyone as generously as you'd cover your own family.

Obamacare also imposes a pesky new excise tax requirement on MERPs called the "Patient Centered Outcomes Research Trust Fund Fee," or PCORI fee. For plans operating in 2018, that amount is projected to be around $2.40 per person, reported on IRS Form 720, and due by July 31, 2018.

Yes, you heard that right. $2.40. You can't even buy a decent cup of coffee for that much. But the statutory penalty for failing to file that report can be as high as $10,000. And while it's not likely the IRS will ever actually impose that fine, you probably want to make sure you dot your "i's" and cross your "t's."

Health Savings Accounts

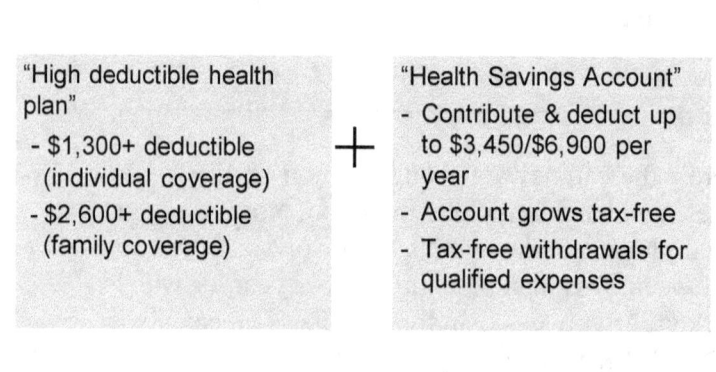

Health Savings Account

"High deductible health plan"
- $1,300+ deductible (individual coverage)
- $2,600+ deductible (family coverage)

$+$

"Health Savings Account"
- Contribute & deduct up to $3,450/$6,900 per year
- Account grows tax-free
- Tax-free withdrawals for qualified expenses

If a Medical Expense Reimbursement Plan isn't appropriate – either because you don't have a spouse to hire, or you have non-family employees you would have to cover – consider establishing a Health Savings Account. These arrangements combine a high-deductible health plan with a tax-free savings account to cover unreimbursed costs.

To qualify, you'll need to be covered by a "high deductible health plan." This means the deductible is at least $1,300 for single coverage or $2,600 for family coverage. Neither you nor your spouse can be covered by a *"non*-high deductible health plan" or by Medicare. The plan can't cover any expense, other than certain preventive care benefits, until you satisfy the annual deductible. You're not eligible if you're covered by a separate plan or rider offering prescription drug benefits before the minimum annual deductible is satisfied.

Once you've established your eligibility, you can open a deductible "health savings account" to cover out-of-pocket expenses not covered by your insurance. For 2018, you can contribute up to $3,450 if you have individual coverage or $6,900 if you have family coverage. (If you're 55 or older, you can save an extra $1,000 per year.)

HSAs are easy to open. Most banks, brokerage firms, and insurance companies offer them. Many times you can even get a debit card to charge expenses directly to the account.

Once you're up and running, you can use your account for most kinds of health insurance, including COBRA continuation and long-term care (but not "Medigap" coverage). You can also use it for the same sort of expenses as a MERP – copays, deductibles, prescriptions, and other out-of-pocket costs.

Withdrawals are tax-free so long as you use them for "qualified medical costs." Withdrawals *not* used for qualified medical costs are subject to regular income tax plus a 20% penalty.

After your death, your account passes to your specified beneficiary. If your beneficiary is your spouse, they can treat it as their own HSA. If not, your beneficiary will pay ordinary tax on the account proceeds (but not the 20% penalty).

The Health Savings Account isn't quite as powerful or flexible as the MERP. You've got specific dollar limits on what you can contribute to the account, which might not match your out-of-pocket costs. And there's no self-employment tax advantage as there is with a MERP. But Health Savings Accounts can still help cut your overall health-care costs by giving you bigger tax deductions.

Flexible Spending Accounts

Flexible spending accounts ("FSAs") let you set aside pre-tax dollars for a variety of nontaxable fringe benefits, including health and disability insurance and medical expense reimbursement. Plan contributions avoid federal income and FICA tax.

The new Obamacare rules let you contribute up to $2,600 per year to your account. Before Obamacare, there were no contribution limits at all. Many observers have called the new $2,600 limit a tax in disguise, especially for older workers with expensive prescriptions who tend to stuff more into their accounts.

Once the money is in the account, you can use it for most medical expenses. However, nonprescription drugs and supplies, long-term care coverage, and associated expenses are not eligible FSA expenses.

Your employer deducts plan contributions from your paycheck and deposits them into your account until you claim your reimbursements.

When you enroll, you have to choose how much to contribute each pay period. You generally can't change your contribution amount in the middle of the plan year unless there's a change in your "family status." Eligible changes include marriage or divorce; birth, adoption, or death of a child; spousal employment; change in a dependent's student status; and the like.

You can claim your full year's reimbursement as soon as you incur qualifying expenses, whether you've fully funded your account for that amount or not.

Historically, FSA rules have required you to use your account balance by the end of the year or forfeit it. However, many employers' plans have taken advantage of a subsequent ruling that lets them amend their plans to provide a 2½ month grace period immediately following the end of the year.

8. Missing a Home Office

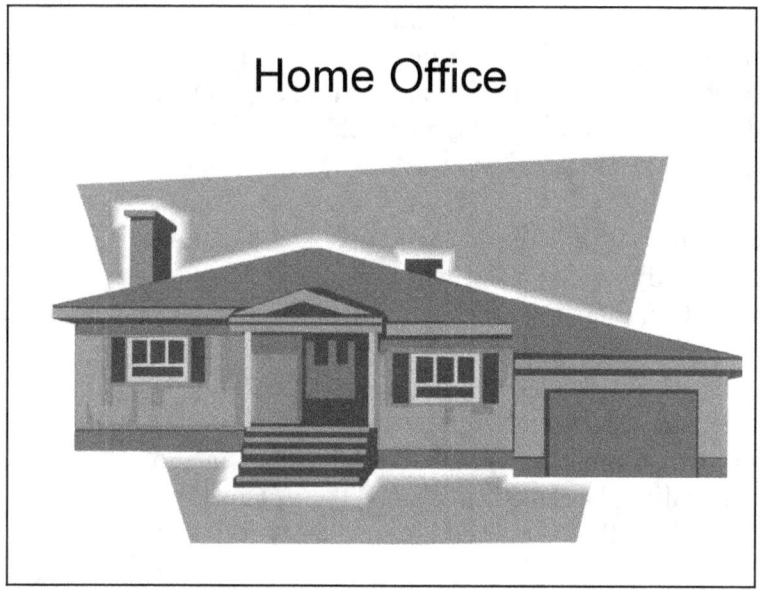

Home office expenses are probably the most misunderstood deduction in the entire tax code. For years, taxpayers feared it guaranteed them an audit. Plenty of tax professionals were happy to go along with that myth. (Maybe they thought it made their jobs easier!) But the U.S. Supreme Court made it easier to qualify for the deduction back in 1994, and Congress made it even easier in 2007. So now your deduction is far less likely to attract attention.

Your home office is deductible if:

- It's your "principal place of business,"

- You use it to meet clients, patients, or prospects in the normal course of your trade or business, or

- It's a separate structure not attached to your dwelling unit.

Most deductible home offices qualify under Rule #1. IRS Publication 587 says your home office qualifies as your principal place of business if:

1. you use it "exclusively and regularly for administrative or management activities of your trade or business," *and*

2. "you have no other fixed location where you conduct substantial administrative or management activities of your trade or business."

This is true even if you have another office, so long as you don't use it more than occasionally for administrative or management activities.

> **Example**: You're a real estate agent and you have a desk at your broker's office. Your *home* office qualifies as your principal place of business so long as you use it to manage your business and keep your books, and you don't regularly do that at your desk at the broker.

Your home office doesn't have to be an entire room. You can use part of a room as long as it meets the requirements. You can also claim a workshop, a studio, or any other "separately identifiable" space you use to store products or samples. If you use it for more than one business, both have to qualify to take the deduction.

You have to use your office regularly and exclusively for business. "Regularly" generally means 10-12 hours per week. To prove your deduction, keep a log and take photos to record your business use.

Once you've qualified, you can start deducting expenses. If your business is taxed as a proprietorship, you'll use Form 8829. If you're taxed as a partnership or corporation, there's no separate form, which helps you "fly under the radar."

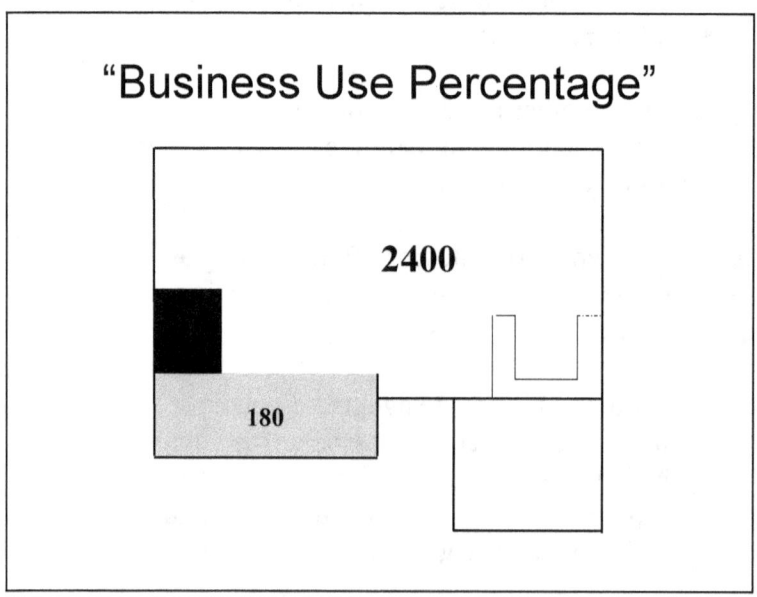

"Business Use Percentage"

2400

180

- Start by calculating the "business use percentage" of your home. You can divide by the number of rooms if they're roughly equal, or calculate the exact percentage of the home's square footage the office occupies. If you use the second method, you can exclude common areas like halls and stairs to boost the overall business use percentage.

- Next, you'll deduct your business use percentage of your rent or your mortgage interest and property taxes. (Deducting those expenses on your business return can save you more than on your personal return. For example, if your state and local taxes are higher than $10,000, you'll sidestep that limit for the portion of property taxes attributable to the home office.

- You'll depreciate the business use percentage of your home's basis (excluding land) over 39 years as nonresidential property.

- Finally, you'll deduct your business use percentage of utilities, repairs, insurance, garbage pickup, and security.

Are there any expenses you can allocate directly to your home office? Maybe you spent extra to renovate the room itself. Maybe you have especially high electric bills for home office equipment? You can claim those as "direct" expenses.

You can also deduct the cost of furnishing, carpeting, and decorating your home office. But be reasonable! If you buy a Picasso at auction, you don't get to deduct it just because it's in your office!

You can use home office expenses to reduce taxable income and self-employment income from your business, but not below zero. If your home office expenses in a particular year are more than your net income from your business, you can carry forward the loss to future years.

When you sell your home, you'll have to recapture any depreciation you claimed or could have claimed after May 6, 1997. You can still claim the usual $250,000 or $500,000 tax-free exclusion for space you use for your office unless it's a "separate dwelling unit."

If this all seems like too much work, there's a new "safe harbor" method that lets you claim a flat $5 per square foot (regardless of your actual expenses) for up to 300 square feet of qualifying home office space (regardless of what percentage it occupies in your home). If you use the safe harbor, you'll continue to deduct your mortgage interest and property tax on Schedule A. However, you'll forego any depreciation deduction. And if the safe harbor deduction reduces your business income below zero, there's no carrying forward the loss.

The safe harbor is certainly easier than the traditional method. However, using it might not let you claim nearly as much as the traditional method. The only way to know is to run the numbers and calculate the deduction both ways.

Claiming a home office can also boost your car and truck deductions. That's because it can minimize or even eliminate nondeductible commuting miles for that business.

> **Example**: You're a real estate agent with a desk at your broker's office. If you don't have a home office, your trip from home to the office is a nondeductible commute. However, if you have a home office, and you start your workday in that office, your "commute" is the trip to the home office, and your trip from home to your desk at the broker is a deductible trip from one business location to another.

9. Missing Car & Truck Expenses

Now let's talk about the most common mistake that business owners and professionals make with vehicle expenses – specifically, calculating them the wrong way.

You know that you can calculate your "actual expenses" for operating your vehicle. Or you can use a much easier standard allowance. For 2018, the allowance is 54.5 cents per mile. Sounds pretty good, right? Well, it might surprise you to see how much it *really* costs to operate your car. And it's almost *never* 54.5 cents per mile!

Every year, AAA researches vehicle operating costs. As the table below shows, if you're taking the standard deduction for a car that costs more than 54.5 cents/mile, you're losing money every time you turn the key.

Vehicle	Cents/Mile
Small Sedan	46.4
Medium Sedan	58.9
Large Sedan	72.2
4WD SUV	73.6
Minivan	65.0

Figures assume 15,000 miles/year $2.86 /gallon gas

Your first step involves calculating your "business use percentage" (BUP) for your vehicle. The IRS divides your trips into three categories: 1) business; 2) commuting; and 3) personal. Ordinary commuting and personal trips are nondeductible. Trips from home to your first business stop and trips from your last business stop to home are personal. (Daily trips to the bank, post office, and similar stops where you perform no service don't qualify as "business.")

Oh, and because you'll ask – yes, you can deduct the cost of plastering your name and logo on your vehicle. But the IRS specifically says it won't convert personal or commuting miles into deductible business miles. Sorry!

Now that we know what qualifies as "business" miles, the IRS gives you four ways to track them. All four require you to keep "adequate records or other sufficient evidence" to support your business use. This means logging mileage at least weekly and keeping receipts for all expenses over $75.

1. **"Brute Force" method:** Record every business mile you drive for the year. Divide your business mileage by your total mileage for the year to calculate BUP. (If you use more than one car for business, this is the method you have to use. I know, what a hassle.)

2. **"90 days" method:** Record your business miles for a "typical" 90-day period. Divide that amount by your total mileage for that period to calculate BUP, then use that percentage for the entire year.

3. **"First Week" method:** Record your business miles for the first week each month. Divide that by your total miles for that period and use it for the entire month.

4. **"Simplified" method:** Record your starting and ending mileage for a 90-day period. Record your personal and commuting miles for that period, and assume all the *rest* of your miles are for business. Calculate your BUP and use it for the entire year. (This is the easiest method if most of your miles are for business.)

Travel between temporary business stops is deductible. So, for example, if you leave home, make six business stops, meet a prospect for dinner, then drive home, your mileage between your first stop and the restaurant is deductible. However, if you have a regular business stop (one that you make at least 8 to 10 times in a six-month period) that you expect to last less than a year, you can count those as business miles, too. If home is your principal place of business, then all business trips are deductible.

Once you've calculated your BUP, you have two ways to calculate your deduction.

1. The **mileage allowance** – the flat 54.5 cents/mile for 2018, *plus* parking, tolls, and your BUP of interest on your car loan and state and local personal property tax on the vehicle. (While we're at it, the allowance for charitable use of the vehicle is capped at just 14 cents/mile, and for medical and moving use, 23.5 cents/mile.)

2. The **"actual expense"** method, where you deduct your full BUP of all expenses. These include:

    *   Depreciation and interest (if you've bought),

    *   Lease payments (if you've leased),

    *   Insurance,

    *   Gasoline, oil, and car washes,

    *   Tires, maintenance, repairs,

    *   License and registration fees,

    *   Personal property tax payments, and

    *   Parking and tolls.

Which one saves the most? Easy – try them both and see. Generally, the more you drive, the more the allowance saves. That's because the allowance assumes 14 cents/mile for depreciation – and as your miles climb, that "assumed" amount can be far more than your actual depreciation. If you're a real road warrior, logging 30,000 or more business miles per year, you'll almost certainly come out ahead with the allowance, no matter what you drive

Okay. What if you've been taking the mileage allowance (because it's easier, or because your tax preparer told you it was all the same), and you discover you ought to be taking actual expenses. What now? Well, if you're taking the allowance now, you *can* switch to the "actual expense" method *if* you own your car – but not if you lease.

Unfortunately, the reverse isn't true. You can't switch from actual expenses to the mileage allowance. You also can't use the allowance if you use five or more vehicles in your business, or you use your vehicle for hire (taxi, Lyft, Uber, etc.).

10. Missing Meals and Entertainment

Now let's take a minute to discuss some fun deductions for meals and entertainment.

The concept here is that you can deduct the cost of meals you host with a bona fide business purpose. This means conversations with clients, prospects, referral sources, and business colleagues. And let me ask you – when do you ever eat with someone who's *not* a client, prospect, referral source, or business colleague? If you're in a business like real estate, insurance, or investments, where you're marketing yourself, the answer might be "never." Be as inclusive as you can with what you define as bona fide business discussion!

The general rule is, you can deduct 50% of your meals, so long as they aren't "lavish or extraordinary." The IRS knows you have to eat, so you can't deduct it *all*.
But they'll meet you halfway. You can deduct the cost of food, drinks, taxes, and tips. (Yes, that includes the coat check and valet parker.)

You generally can't deduct the cost of meals you eat with your spouse unless you're traveling together for business. However, you can include the cost of a spouse or other "closely connected" person if your guest brings *their* spouse.

Documenting expenses is probably easier than you think. You don't need receipts for expenses under $75. But you do need to record five pieces of information in your business diary or records. (Credit card statements work for the first three as long as you corroborate them with the fourth and fifth in some sort of diary or log):

1. How much you spent

2. When you spent it

3. Where you spent it

4. Your business relationship with your guest (prospect, client, referral source, vendor, etc.)

5. The business purpose of the meal

Do you entertain at home? Do you ever discuss business when you do? (Of course.) Are you deducting those meals, too? (Probably not.) There's no requirement that you have to eat *out* to deduct the costs of a meal. So don't forget to deduct home entertainment expenses too! If you invite up to a dozen guests, use the same rules as if you were eating out. If you invite more than 12 guests, you can deduct "reasonable" costs if your primary purpose is business. Include employees; let guests know your business purpose; discuss and display your product or service to support your deduction.

You can also deduct off-premises meals you provide as part of required business meetings.

You can deduct 100%, rather than the usual 50%, of your expenses for meals and entertainment for sales seminars and similar events where the meal is integral to the presentation or the business. (If you're a Somali pirate, for example, you can deduct 100% of the cost of meals you provide to crews you hold hostage on your ship.)

Now here's some bad news. It used to be that you could also deduct entertainment expenses for events like ball games, movies, or concerts, if they took place directly before or after substantial, bona fide discussion directly related to the active conduct of your business. You could deduct the face value of tickets to events, food and drinks, parking, taxes, and tips.

At least, you *could*. The Tax Cuts and Jobs Act of 2017 eliminates that deduction.

While we're on the topic of hospitality, let's talk about business gifts. Gifts you give to business associates are deductible up to $25 if you can show a business purpose for the expense or business benefit to be gained. (Married couples count as one person for this rule—you can't deduct $25 for each.) This includes your family and friends if they qualify as bona fide clients, prospects, or referral sources. Gifts are nontaxable to the recipient.

- If you give a gift to a group of recipients, such as a family or an office, you can deduct $25 for each member of the group.

- Advertising specialties like pens and other tchotchkes with a value up to $4 each are deductible as advertising expenses and don't count against the $25 per person annual limit for business gifts. Contest prizes you give to customers (but not employees) also qualify.

11. Missing *My* Help

Now that you see how business owners miss out on tax breaks, let's talk about the final mistake. And that is (drumroll, please) failing to take advantage of *my* help.

Way back in Chapter One, I talked about how most tax professionals drive using the rearview mirror. They do a perfectly decent job recording the history *you* give them – but they don't do much, if anything, to help you write a new history – one that costs you less in the taxes we all hate to pay.

In the course of reading this book, you've probably found some things you aren't doing as effectively as you could be. Maybe you're operating your business in the wrong entity. Maybe you're missing a home office deduction you really deserve. Maybe you're missing out on car and truck deductions, or meals and entertainment.

And you probably haven't done *any* real *planning* at all. (That's OK – most of my new clients haven't, simply because they don't realize how important it really is.)

If that's the case, then isn't it about time you stop driving in the rearview mirror? Isn't it time you stop settling for just recording history?

That's where *I* come in.

I give you the plan you need to stop wasting thousands of dollars in tax you don't have to pay.

I'll sit down with you and your most recent returns. I'll take the time to walk through those returns, item by item by item. I'll look at how you make your money and where you spend it. Then I'll tie it all together in a comprehensive *plan* that helps you accomplish your goals in the most tax-efficient way possible.

You'll be satisfied knowing you're doing everything the law allows to get that tax bill off your back. And you'll rest easy knowing everything we recommend is court-tested and IRS-approved.

I can't promise how much you'll save until we sit down with you and your returns. But I can promise you'll save more than if you keep driving with the rearview mirror!

So please, call me with your questions. Come to me for a *plan*. You have nothing to lose but taxes, and possibly thousands to gain. Why would you wait to make that call?

Steve Bibisi

Kingdom Financial Solutions

1921 Boston Post Road

Westbrook, CT 06498

860.490.9741

Questions and Notes

Questions and Notes

_____

_____

_____

_____

_____

_____

_____

_____

_____

_____

_____

_____

_____

_____

_____

_____

_____

_____

_____

_____

_____

_____

_____

_____

_____

_____

Kingdom Financial Solutions